THE Publishing Company Presents

The Secrets to

Renewing Your Mind

&

Walking in the Perfect Will of God

Table of Contents

RENEW YOUR MIND 3

NECESSITY OF A RENEWED MIND 4

GOD'S INTELLIGENCE IS AVAILABLE 9

YOU ARE IN CONTROL 17

DAY AND NIGHT...21

MIND GOD'S WILL...26

JESUS IS GOD'S WILL 33

FEEL LIKE WALKING LIKE JESUS..39

SET YOUR MIND...44

PARTNER WITH US 51

Renew Your Mind

In this book we are going to cover what it looks like to renew your mind, using God's Word in collaboration with the Spirit of God. The Bible says that we are not to conform to the patterns we see in this world, but instead we are to be transformed by the renewing of our minds. When your mind is transformed by the Word of God, it actually puts you on the correct path in life. If you remember in Deuteronomy 30:15, Moses gives the people two different paths in life, he says,

See, I have set before you today life and good, death and evil...

He says there is one path you could take that will lead to destruction, cursing and every awful thing that you could imagine. Then there is another path that leads to blessing, prosperity and having success in every area of your life. He lays out those two paths before the people and he says it is up to us which path we take. A lot of people get caught up in the sovereignty of God but they forget about the responsibility of man. Man is responsible for what he does with the tools that God gives him. That's you and I. God's Word is a tool in our life, as well as the empowerment of His Holy Spirit, to go and do the works of the ministry, to walk out changed lives, to be set free from sin, and to go from mountaintop to mountaintop, success to success, victory to victory, and strength to strength in all that we do.

The Bible says we are more than conquerors through Christ. That means we don't have losses. We don't go backwards. The devourer is rebuked for our sake. Therefore we go from victory to victory. But you must have a renewed mind by the Word of God in order to live an enabled life of victory. I want you to believe it right now in your heart. Say it out loud,

I will be transformed by the Word of God.

Necessity of a Renewed Mind

The most important part of living a life with a renewed mind is understanding that your mind needs to be renewed. The Bible says in 2 Corinthians 5:17 that when you're baptized and you are born again, you put off your old man.

Therefore, if anyone *is* in Christ, *he is* a new creation; old things have passed away; behold, all things have become new.

You put off the old self, and behold, all things become new. That includes your mind. It says that your inheritance in Christ is actually the mind of Christ. But how many of us know that when we get baptized, we give our life to Christ, we don't just wake up with the mind of Christ. It's in us. All of God's promises are in us. The kingdom of God is in us. The Holy Spirit is in us, but we have to push all of the carnality out, and that happens by the renewing of God's Word.

We are going to go through a lot of scripture, you are going to be fed the Word through this whole book, and it is going to get you out of a any remaining victimhood mentality. If there's one way to really sum up people in America, it's that they live constantly victimized. People in America get caught in this trap thinking that they are the victim in every situation because they haven't been taught how to renew their mind into a position of authority in Christ. It says in Ephesians chapter one that all authority has been given to Christ on heaven, on earth, and below the earth, and God has delegated it to the Church, which is his body. It says,

Far above all principality, and power, and might, and dominion, and every name that is named, not only in this world, but also in that which is to come: And hath put all things under his feet,

and gave him to be the head over all things to the church, which is his body, the fulness of him that filleth all in all.

We are the Church, and it says that all of the power in the heavenly places is under our feet. But if you don't understand that, and your mind is not renewed, then you can't live in a lifestyle of victory.
But when you read this teaching, and get it in your spirit, there will not be one area in your life that you could ever be victimized ever again. I want you to say this out loud,

I will never be a victim again.

Just because bad things happen to you doesn't mean you have to dwell on them. It doesn't mean they become your reality. It doesn't mean that they change your circumstances. Something crazy can happen, but it even says in Genesis 50:20 that what the devil intends for evil in your life God actually flips for good. It says,

Far above all principality, and power, and might, and dominion, and every name that is named, not only in this world, but also in that which is to come, and hath put all things under his feet, and gave him to be the head over all things to the church, which is his body, the fulness of him that filleth all in all.

So when you know how to recognize and identify that there are attacks of the devil coming into your life, you can spot them out and declare the Word of God over them. You can say, "Thanks devil, that you've tried to be a giant in my life, but the same way that David took down Goliath, God is going to take you down, right now, even by my words!" You speak like that to giants in your life. You speak like that to situations in your life. You choose today to draw a line in the sand and say,

I won't be a victim anymore. My mind will be renewed and I will walk in victory, in Jesus's mighty name!

Your mind must be renewed. What it means to be renewed is that it cannot stay the way that it is. The way you think right now can't remain. The way you see the world right now can't remain. The way you perceive the world and recognize circumstances cannot stay the same, it must always be renewed. In the book of Romans chapter 12 starting in verse 1 says,

I beseech you therefore, brethren, by the mercies of God, that ye present your bodies a living sacrifice, holy, acceptable unto God, which is your reasonable service. And be not conformed to this world: but be ye transformed by the renewing of your mind, that ye may prove what is that good, and acceptable, and perfect, will of God.

What is good and acceptable and perfect? Understanding this is key. First, you must understand that you are a spirit. You are not your mind. You are not your soul. That's what modern psychology will get you to think, that your identity is wrapped up in your feelings, but that's not true! That's not the truth. Your identity is not wrapped up in your feelings, or it shouldn't be. You are a spirit. The Bible says you are an eternal spirit, you have a mind, which is your soul. You have a soul, which is your mind, your will, your emotions, your intellect, your free will, and your emotions are the overflow of your mind, and you live in a body. You are a spirit, you possess a soul, and you live in a body.

Where a lot of Christians get caught up is their soul possesses them instead of them possessing their soul. Your mind is not in control of you. You are in control of your mind. That revelation alone will change everything in your life! Your mind does not control you, you were created to control your mind. Your mind is actually a tool given to you by God to function as the hands and feet of Jesus in this life, and to live an abundant life.

What fuels your mind is God's Word if you do it appropriately. Whatever gets into your mind through your eyes and through your ears is what your soul is fueled by. That's why the Bible says to not conform to the patterns of this world. When you watch Netflix series, when you listen to crazy podcasts, crazy music, you are fueling your mind according to the patterns of this world. What you watch and what you listen to ultimately determines the state of your mind, your will, and your emotions. The bible says to be renewed. I want you to say that and understand this:

I don't conform to the direction that everyone else in this world is going. I am renewed by God's Word.

Understand that you are in control of your mind, your mind is not in control of you. Ephesians chapter 4 starting in verse 17 says,

This I say therefore, and testify in the Lord, that ye henceforth walk not as other Gentiles walk, in the vanity of their mind, having the understanding darkened, being alienated from the life of God through the ignorance that is in them, because of the blindness of their heart.

The Gentiles did not know God's law. They were not renewed in their minds. Paul is saying here, "Don't walk as somebody who has not renewed in their mind. You must be renewed in your mind." They were darkened in their understanding, alienated from the life of God because of the ignorance that was in them, due to their hardness of heart. They had become callous and had given themselves up to sensuality, greed. to practice every kind of impurity. But that is not the way you learned Christ. The truth in Jesus is to put off your old self, which belongs to your former manner of life and is corrupt, through deceitful desires, and to be renewed in the spirit of your minds. To put on the new self, created after the likeness of God, in true righteousness and true holiness.

What do you see oftentimes in Christian circles when this isn't taught and preached in the church? You'll see Christians that live a life confessing Christ, but they have no outward appearance of the fruit of God working in their life, of God's Word working in their life. They're still living in depression and anxiety, in addiction, stuck in the bondage of sin. There's no freedom in their life yet. They're going to church every Sunday thinking that's what makes them a Christian, because they're ignorant just like it says here in Ephesians chapter 4. They're ignorant of the fact that there's freedom for them, that they can be renewed from the inside out. The devil will try to put lies and thoughts and carnality above Christ. The flesh will try to exalt itself above Christ, but we do not allow that to happen. The Bible says instead to put off the old self and to put on the new life which is the righteousness of God, being renewed in the spirit of your mind. You are renewed in the spirit of your mind by God's Word, and God's righteousness. The Bible says in John chapter 15:3,

You are already clean because of the word which I have spoken to you.

God's Word actually cleans your mind. It cleans your thoughts, it cleans your imagination, it cleans your vision, it cleans your desires. God's Word washes over you and renews you from the inside out. The Bible says in Proverbs 23:7,

…For as he thinks in his heart, so is he.

Your thoughts actually determine your life. Your thoughts determine your steps. Your thoughts determine your words. Your thoughts determine the entire progression of your life. So it's crucial that a man's thought life is put into alignment with God's Word, and when your thoughts are put into alignment with God's Word you will walk out the perfect, acceptable and good will of God for your life. If you want to walk in God's perfect will for your life say this outloud,

I know God's will for my life. God's Word is His will and I will walk out His word in my life.

I want you to say that out loud wherever you're at, believe it and speak it. That's what the spirit of faith does! Amen! So number one, you must be renewed in your mind by the washing and renewing and transforming of God's Word.

God's Intelligence is Available

Number two, you must understand that God's intelligence is available to us. What is intelligence? Intelligence is a culmination of wisdom and knowledge. So God's wisdom and God's knowledge is available to you. If you don't understand that then you will have no desire to be renewed in your mind. But when you have revelation of that fact, that God's wisdom and God's knowledge is available to you, then you will go and seek it out.

The Bible says in Proverbs 25:2,

It is the glory of God to conceal a matter, but the glory of kings *is* to search out a matter.

When you have the revelation that God has secrets to success, God has spiritual laws laid out in His Word, and God has the secret oracles that will put you in a position of victory in this life, in freedom, then you'll actually have a zeal and a passion to go seek those out. You must understand God's wisdom and God's knowledge is available to you at any time, but it comes through revelation.

Revelation comes through hunger and thirst. You must hunger and thirst for God's revelation.. Through that hunger and thirst, and then by hearing and understanding, God provides revelation for you and that revelation is what renews your mind. Go with me to 1 Corinthians chapter 2:6-10,

We do, however, speak a message of wisdom among the mature, but not the wisdom of this age or of the rulers of this age, who are coming to nothing. No, we declare God's wisdom, a mystery that has been hidden and that God destined for our

glory before time began. None of the rulers of this age understood it, for if they had, they would not have crucified the Lord of glory. However, as it is written: **What no eye has seen, what no ear has heard, and what no human mind has conceived the things God has prepared for those who love him these are the things God has revealed to us by his Spirit. The Spirit searches all things, even the deep things of God.**

I believe if you're reading this you are a mature Christian. You are looking for maturity, you are seeking to go deeper, you are looking to go higher. You want to go further, you want to know more, you want more revelation, you want more of the anointing, you want more of God's presence, you want more access to God and to His wisdom. That is what makes a mature Christian. A humble Christian is a mature Christian. Somebody who never thinks they've made it. They never get arrogant, they never get prideful, they never think, "All right, I've made it to the top, I can kick back and relax." No, they are a hungry Christian who reads books like this and listens to God's Word as it goes forth. That makes you a mature Christian. Read again,

However, as it is written: What no eye has seen, what no ear has heard, and what no human mind has conceived the things God has prepared for those who love him these are the things God has revealed to us by his Spirit.

There are things that you can't even see, there are things you haven't even heard, there are things that haven't gotten into your heart yet, that God will reveal to you if you're willing to be renewed in your mind. 1 Corinthians 2:10-11 says,

These things God has revealed to us through the Spirit. For the Spirit searches everything, even the depths of God. For who knows a person's thoughts except the spirit of that person, which is in him? So also no one comprehends the thoughts of God except the Spirit of God.

Because the Spirit of God comprehends the thoughts of God, and we are the temple of God's Spirit, we have the mind and the thoughts of God. Now tell me this, if God is living in you, and He's given you His thoughts, He's given you access to His wisdom and His knowledge, would God ever fail in life? Would God ever go backwards in life? Would God ever not see success in something that He does? No! So we align ourselves with God's Word, and we believe it, we stand on it, we speak it and we thank Him for it. Say this out loud,

Thank you Lord that your Word says that your Spirit is in me, your Spirit searches the depths of your heart and your mind and you impart to me your wisdom and your knowledge to go forward and to conquer giants, to move mountains, to build the biggest churches on the planet, to get more people saved, to feed more hungry people, to overcome the world.

You name it, and that's what God's wisdom and God's knowledge will shed abroad in you. And you, by His Spirit will do what He places in your Spirit to do! That's why God told Abraham in Deuteronomy 26:19,

And that He will set you high above all nations which He has made, in praise, in name, and in honor, and that you may be a holy people to the Lord your God, just as He has spoken.

Now go back to 1 Corinthians 2:12-13,

What we have received is not the spirit of the world, but the Spirit who is from God, so that we may understand what God has freely given us. This is what we speak, not in words taught us by human wisdom but in words taught by the Spirit, explaining spiritual realities with Spirit-taught words.

So you must be spiritual in order to receive the teachings of spiritual truths. That's why you will go into a massive amount of religious churches these days, and they're not spiritual, renewed, or living in total victory. They refuse to be spiritual.

They're not baptized in the Holy Ghost, so they get stuck saying the Apostles Creed and repeating documents and things that they've been taught for forever and ever. And the moment that you go in there and ruffle some feathers, they get mad at you and they say, "This is how we've done it ever since my great-great-grandma Ludacris or whatever her name is did it." That'd be a funny name for a great-great-grandma. She probably has a gold chain and a couple gold teeth. But that's what happens! You will go into religious circles and do something according to the Word of God, and if it goes against their tradition, it ruffles their feathers. It's because they're not spiritual. Only spiritual people can gather what the Spirit of the Lord is saying. Continue to verse 14,

The person without the Spirit does not accept the things that come from the Spirit of God but considers them foolishness, and cannot understand them because they are discerned only through the Spirit. The person with the Spirit makes judgments about all things, but such a person is not subject to merely human judgments, for who has known the mind of the Lord so as to instruct him? But we have the mind of Christ.

I want you to say this out loud,

I have the mind of Christ! I am spiritual! I have the mind of Christ!

Again, if you have the mind of Christ, is there any area of your life that you should go backwards in? Or should you constantly progress and go higher? See increase? Experience more love, more power, more anointing, more wisdom, more knowledge, more souls saved? Every area of your life, with the mind of Christ, should be unstoppable. Now don't get me wrong, we are not here to build an earthly kingdom. We are here to build a heavenly kingdom. But you see how God called Abraham and He said, "You were one man when I called you, and I made you a mighty Nation." The power that is in you as a Christian, that can reside in your mind by the renewing of your mind, is unstoppable. It is unstoppable!

This means you don't have to wander around like a chicken with your head cut off like a lot of people do. If you look at many people, they look like zombies, even if they are dressed up in church. That's why it says in the gospels that Jesus had compassion on people, because He saw the people and they were as sheep without a shepherd. When you get a hold of God's wisdom and God's knowledge, you are no longer running around like a sheep without a shepherd.

Jesus said, "My sheep know my voice." God's voice is His Word. You know the voice of God. When you know the Word of God, you know the voice of God. And when you know the voice of Jesus, then you're not going to wander around like a sheep without a shepherd. That is so crucial when it comes to the topic of renewing your mind, because the Bible explains that the world is going in one direction, that there's a pattern of this world, and then there is a pattern of the Kingdom of God.

The Bible says in Hosea 4:6,

My people are destroyed for lack of knowledge...

God didn't say that the devil destroys His people, or that enemies in this life destroys them. God didn't say anyone destroys His people except for themselves. He says, "My people destroy themselves because of a lack of knowledge." You get revelation knowledge from the Word and from God's Spirit. So knowledge, on the contrary, eliminates the ability of destruction. With sound knowledge and the renewing of your mind you eliminate the ability to be destroyed. To be destroyed from your enemies, to be destroyed from the devil, to be destroyed from poverty or sickness or disease. Revelation knowledge enables you to not be destroyed.

Let's say you are a general in a war and you are fighting against another army, and you have knowledge of the other general's plan to come and conquer you. If you have knowledge of his plan, who is going to win? You are going to win because you have knowledge of what it is that he has planned to do. So one, you will actually avoid the attack. And two, you will counter the planned attack and you will win! The Bible says there is nothing new under the sun. The devil has the same few tricks, he's got the same schemes, the same lies, the same strategies he's been doing ever since the beginning. When you have knowledge of what the devil is doing, when you know according to knowledge of God the way your enemy moves, you will always win!

When you know God's will for your life, for your finances, for your marriage, for your health, for your church, for your relationships, when you have that knowledge, it enables you to not be destroyed in those areas. But any area of your life where you lack knowledge you open a door to the possibility of destruction. Understand this and say this out loud,

Any area of my life that my lack knowledge, will eventually be destroyed.

The devil is aiming to destroy your whole life. So any area of your life where you lack knowledge, he will eventually destroy. But if you get God's Word in you, you will receive all the knowledge of God, and you will always be capable of fending off the enemy.

How do you get knowledge the Word of God? The Bible says you have the mind of Christ, and if Jesus's mind is in you, now you have access to the very thoughts of God. You spend time with Him, you fast, you pray, you spend time in His Word. God's will is his Word. God's blessing begins where His will is known, so when you know God's will, that's where his blessing begins in your life. That's where faith begins in your life. Faith begins where the will of God is known.

Look at Proverbs 4:5-9,

Get wisdom! Get understanding! Do not forget, nor turn away

from the words of my mouth. Do not forsake her, and she will preserve you; Love her, and she will keep you. Wisdom *is* the principal thing; *Therefore* get wisdom. And in all your getting, get understanding. Exalt her, and she will promote you; She will bring you honor, when you embrace her. She will place on your head an ornament of grace; A crown of glory she will deliver to you.

There are promises attached to these actions. When you get understanding and you don't forsake her, she will keep you in wisdom, she will guard you. Wisdom will exalt you and honor you if you embrace her. There are promises tied to wisdom and knowledge, and a lack thereof opens the door for destruction. But wisdom actually exalts you. God exalts you according to your revelation of His wisdom and the Word. Notice it says,

And in all your getting, get understanding.

Understand the wisdom of God, get revelation, meditate on it. You can get God's intelligence for every area of life. There is an answer for every question in the Word of God. I heard this story about a man who was an investor, he loved to invest. He made a ton of money investing and he would go into his closet every day and he would pray to God about the different investments that he had written down. He would get into his closet and say, "Lord, this is what's on the chart today, here are my options, where should I put my money? Where should I invest?" And he would pray over his investments. God would give him an answer, and every time God spoke to him he always made money. He never lost money! He just increased and increased until he became a very wealthy man, because he received knowledge and wisdom from God, according to his Word. He spent time in prayer with Him, listened to the voice of God, and acted on it. That is available to every person! Lift your hands to the Lord and say this out loud,

From this day forward, the wisdom and knowledge of God is going to flood my life in every area of my being. I'm going to walk in fresh revelation, fresh knowledge and fresh wisdom from this day forward. I am going to know the insights and oracles of God, in Jesus's mighty name!

To review so far, we must be renewed in our mind, and God's intelligence, His wisdom and knowledge, is available to us by His Word.

You Are In Control

The third lesson to learn about renewing your mind, is that you are in control of your mind. I want you to really get this, and I want you to say this out loud,

I am in control of my mind.

You have to understand that your mind is not in control of you, you are in control of your mind. You are not your thoughts. You are not what you think about. When you get hungry, you think about cheeseburgers. Are you a cheeseburger? No, you're not! You are not your thoughts. You have authority to control your thoughts. Your soul, your mind, your will and your emotions were given to you as tools by God, to be renewed by his Word, and to give you the ability to walk as Christ walked in this earth. Your mind is a tool given to you by God. It does not control you, you control your mind. It eliminates your ability to become a victim when you understand this.

Declare this over yourself,

I am in control of my mind, I am in control of what gets in my mind. I am in control of, and responsible for what I think on, what comes out of my mouth, and what gets in my heart.

When people take responsibility for that, all of a sudden it removes victimhood from any situation. That's why a lot of Christians don't like to teach on this or believe it, because it puts them in a position to where they have to act on it. And the moment that you are required to act on your faith, you have to put your big boy pants on. But I know that if you are reading this right now, you have your big boy pants on, amen!

The reality is, crazy thoughts are going to pop up, weird things are going to happen, lies are going to come your way, the devil is going to try to whisper thing to you. Fleshly thoughts are going to pop up here and there because you still battle against the flesh in this life. You have to understand the difference between a carnal thought, or what is coming from your flesh, and what is the spiritual thought, what is coming from your spirit. When you can discern and separate what is coming from the flesh and what's coming from the spirit, you can cast down fleshly thoughts and make them submit to your spirit.

Go to 2 Corinthians 10:3-5,

For though we walk in the flesh, we do not war according to the flesh. For the weapons of our warfare *are* not carnal but mighty in God for pulling down strongholds, casting down arguments and every high thing that exalts itself against the knowledge of God, bringing every thought into captivity to the obedience of Christ...

A mighty man of God, Keneth E Hagin used to say, "You can't stop birds from flying over your hair or over your head, but you can stop them from building a nest in your hair." There is going to be thoughts that pop up. You can't stop every wild thought from passing through your mind. But you can stop them from building a nest in your mind and taking up residence. So the moment that some crazy thought pops up, you take capture of it, and you exalt Christ above it. You cast it down. You have the authority to do that! Whatever crazy thought comes up, you take a hold of it, and you say, "No, that's not my thought. My thoughts are renewed by God's Word. I'm renewed in my mind."

The Bible says this about even situations where people struggle with lust. If you have a lustful thought that pops up, you get rid of it. You say, "No, that's not me. That's not what I desire. My mind is renewed by God's Word. I flee from youthful passions in Jesus's mighty name!" You plead the blood of Jesus over your mind and you make your carnality submit to your spirit. Make it obedient to Christ. I want you to really understand this, and say it out loud,

Words become thoughts, thoughts become feelings, feelings become actions. Again, words become thoughts, thoughts become feelings, feelings become actions.

Whatever words are getting into your mind will determine what you think, and what you think will ultimately determine how you feel. And how you feel will determine how you act, or how you live. Control what enters your mind through your eyes and through your ears, and you will transform the entire pattern of your life. That is part of what it means to be renewed in your mind. Change the words that get in your mind, and it will change the thoughts that you have, which will change the feelings that you have, which will change the actions that you take. Words become thoughts, thoughts become feelings, and feelings become actions.

We are renewed in our mind by God's Word. When you read teachings like this, watch our live streams, and you get preaching inside of you, it renews your mind. You get pumped full of faith. You hear God's Word. It does something supernatural for you! It cleanses you. Those crazy things that happen throughout your day, they get brushed off. The anointing destroys the yoke of bondage. You come into the anointing and Jesus gives you a light burden, with an easy yoke, and you get pumped full of faith to go and conquer every wicked plan that the devil has against your life. You feel renewed!

The Bible says in Matthew 13:3-9,

Then He spoke many things to them in parables, saying: "Behold, a sower went out to sow. And as he sowed, some *seed* **fell by the wayside; and the birds came and devoured them. Some fell on stony places, where they did not have much earth; and they immediately sprang up because they had no depth of earth. But when the sun was up they were scorched, and because they had no root they withered away. And some fell among thorns, and the thorns sprang up and choked them. But others fell on good ground and yielded a crop: some a hundredfold, some sixty, some thirty. He who has ears to hear, let him hear!"**

The sower sows the Word, so like a farmer, God's Word is a seed. And when you read teachings like this, watch live streams, you are actually planting God's Word into your mind and into your heart. When God's Word gets into your mind and it gets into your heart, it changes you from the inside out, into the very image of Christ. From one level of glory to another level of glory, in Jesus's mighty name! Not from loss to loss, backsliding to backsliding, but from victory to victory, mountain top to mountaintop. Not hills and valleys, but living a steady path going directly up and live in a victorious life in Jesus's mighty name. As more than a conqueror.

You don't even have to fight the battle, you just resist the devil. You put on the armor of God, the helmet of salvation that secures your mind, you lift up the shield of faith, and it quenches all the fiery darts of the devil. You take up the sword of the Spirit, which is the Word of God, and you cut down the lies of the enemy. You take a stand, you draw a line in the sand, and you refuse to go backwards. You are only going forward in Jesus's mighty name! That life of victory only comes by God's Word renewing you in the spirit of your mind.

Day and Night

The fourth main key to renewing your mind, is to meditate on God's Word, day and night. A lot of people ask, "Why do we have day and night services? Why do some preachers have revival meetings in the morning and then they have some revival meetings at night? Why don't we just do church at like you know, 10 in the morning and that's it? Only have one service a day?" No, the Bible says you meditate on the Word day and night. Psalm 1:1-3 says,

Blessed *is* the man who walks not in the counsel of the ungodly, nor stands in the path of sinners, nor sits in the seat of the scornful; but his delight *is* in the law of the LORD, and in His law he meditates day and night. He shall be like a tree planted by the rivers of water, that brings forth its fruit in its season, whose leaf also shall not wither; and whatever he does shall prosper.

When you are meditating on God's Word, when you get preaching into you day and night, all day long, all night long, it renews your mind, and transforms you. I wake up every morning with a song that comes out of my spirit, or scripture, because that is how much of God's Word gets inside me. I'm not joking here, I'm not exaggerating, Every day when I wake up, I wake up and I have something spiritual coming out of my mouth. Your spirit doesn't sleep. Your spirit will pray even as you're asleep. As your flesh sleeps, your spirit man will be praying. I'll wake up in the morning and I'll have a song. "There is power, power, wonder working power, in the blood of the lamb..." I'll just have songs like that flowing out of my spirit when I wake up. That is what it looks like to live a life where you meditate on God's Word day and night. And when you do that, it will get in you and it will be all that will come out of you. When that happens, you know you are living a life of victory. When all that is in you is God's Word and all that comes out of you is God's Word, you are living in victory.

The Bible says in John 1:1,

In the beginning was the Word, and the Word was with God, and the Word was God.

Who was the Word? Jesus became flesh and dwelt among us. That is what it looks like to be revealed into the very image of Christ, from glory to glory. When you know God's Word is in you, and you are meditating on it, it gives you strength. It's life to your bones, it's healing to your flesh, it builds up your faith to go and take a mountain like Caleb did at the age of 85. When God's Word gets inside of you, you are unstoppable with the spirit of faith. With a spirit of faith, meditate on God's Word, and think on these things. The Bible says in Colossians 3:2

Set your mind on things above, not on things on the earth.

The Bible also says in Philippians 4:8,

Finally, brethren, whatsoever things are true, whatsoever things are honest, whatsoever things are just, whatsoever things are pure, whatsoever things are lovely, whatsoever things are of good report; if there be any virtue, and if there be any praise, think on these things.

When you set your mind on the things of Christ and the things of His Word, you are guaranteed to walk in freedom and anointing of success, everywhere you go. Meditate on the Word. This is the same message that the Lord gave Abraham, Moses, Joshua, David and gave to Solomon. It's the same message all the way back from the beginning. The Lord said in Joshua 1:1-9,

Every place that the sole of your foot will tread upon I have given you, as I said to Moses. From the wilderness and this Lebanon as far as the great river, the River Euphrates, all the land of the Hittites, and to the Great Sea toward the going down of the sun, shall be your territory. No man shall *be able to* stand before you all the days of your life; as I was with Moses, *so* I will be with you. I will not leave you nor forsake you.

Be strong and of good courage, for to this people you shall divide as an inheritance the land which I swore to their fathers to give them. Only be strong and very courageous, that you may observe to do according to all the law which Moses My servant commanded you; do not turn from it to the right hand or to the left, that you may prosper wherever you go. This Book of the Law shall not depart from your mouth, but you shall meditate in it day and night, that you may observe to do according to all that is written in it. For then you will make your way prosperous, and then you will have good success. Have I not commanded you? Be strong and of good courage; do not be afraid, nor be dismayed, for the LORD your God *is* with you wherever you go.

That is Go. That is how He thinks. That is how He functions. When you get His Word in you and you meditate on it, that becomes your reality! I want you to say this out loud,

That is my reality in Jesus's mighty name!

The Bible says in Romans 12:2 says.

Do not conform to the pattern of this world, but be transformed by the renewing of your mind. Then you will be able to test and approve what God's will is His good, pleasing and perfect will.

We are not to look like the world. We are not to listen to the same music as the world, watch the same movies as the world, go to the same events as the world. We are called to invade the world, but not to be going in the same direction as the world. When we make that our objective, then we are no longer conformed to the patterns in this world but instead we are transformed in the renewing of our mind. And when we are transformed according to God's wisdom and God's knowledge that we receive, we function on the level of God's intelligence and we live victoriously.

Obviously you get wisdom from all the other books of the Bible as well, but the book of Proverbs holds the wisdom of God. It holds the wisdom of God on renewing your mind. Earlier we talked about intelligence, how God's intelligence, His wisdom and His knowledge is available to you. Proverbs 4:4-6 says,

Then he taught me, and he said to me, "Take hold of my words with all your heart; keep my commands, and you will live. Get wisdom, get understanding; do not forget my words or turn away from them. Do not forsake wisdom, and she will protect you; love her, and she will watch over you.

You need God's wisdom and you need God's knowledge in order to have success in life. So destruction doesn't come upon you. You need wisdom to be exalted in life and your mind must be renewed. You must cast down every thought that attempts to exalt itself above Christ, so every thought that doesn't align with God's Word. God's Word always supersedes any thought that pops into your mind that is against it. So any thought, any feeling that attempts to contradict what God's Word says about you, you begin to stand up and you quote the Word, you praise God. Isaiah 61:3 says,

To appoint unto them that mourn in Zion, to give unto them beauty for ashes, the oil of joy for mourning, the garment of praise for the spirit of heaviness; that they might be called trees of righteousness, the planting of the LORD, that he might be glorified.

When you start thinking negative things, if the devil tries and comes to lie to you and he tells you that you're ugly, you're fat, you're depressed, you're anxious, or you should kill yourself, when all these wicked things attempt to come at you, remember what the Word of God says, and let it overcome those things.

If that's what you've been struggling with today, it broken off of your life right now in Jesus's mighty name. Begin to *believe* God's Word, and then speak it! Say,

I'm fearfully and wonderfully made, in the very image of God. The Bible says I can put on a garment of praise. I praise you Lord, that you've saved me, that I spend eternity with you, that your blood has reconciled me, it has justified me, and it has glorified me. That you sat me at the right hand of Christ, that as you are in this world, so am I, that you destroyed the power of sin in my life, that you put your Spirit in me and you put your Spirit upon me to go about being the hands and feet of Jesus all over the earth.

Start speaking like that, get God's Word in your ears, in your heart and in your mind. Meditate on it, be renewed by it, and you will watch God create doorway after doorway, path after path of success and glory in your life. His glory will be your rear guard. The Bible says in Isaiah 58:8,

Then your light shall break forth like the morning, Your healing shall spring forth speedily, And your righteousness shall go before you; The glory of the LORD shall be your rear guard.

You will eliminate the opportunity for destruction, protected by meditating on the Word of God day and night as you go from faith to faith, glory to glory, and God's glory is your rear guard.

Mind God's Will

God would not be a God of love, unless He gave us the free will to choose Him or to not choose Him. I heard it put this way one time, "God loves you so much, He'll allow you to send yourself to hell." I like how evangelist Tiff Shuttlesworth says it. "God sends nobody to hell. People send themselves to hell because they refuse to receive Jesus Christ as their Lord and savior." God gives you a free will to choose, because true love gives you the ability to choose. So your will is your ability to choose in life. I want you to say that out loud,

My will is my ability to choose.

It is crucial to understand God's will and your will, and how to move your will out of your life and take on God's will for your life. see your will is your ability to choose according to the Bible

Romans chapter 8:5 says,

Those who live according to the flesh have their minds set on what the flesh desires; but those who live in accordance with the Spirit have their minds set on what the Spirit desires.

I want you to say this out loud,

I set my mind on the things of the spirit.

The fifth key to renewing your mind, is deliberately setting your mind on the things of the Spirit. The Bible says to not be carnally minded.

The Bible says in James 3:13-4:1,

Who *is* wise and understanding among you? Let him show by good conduct *that* his works *are done* in the meekness of wisdom. But if you have bitter envy and self-seeking in your hearts, do not boast and lie against the truth. This wisdom does not descend from above, but *is* earthly, sensual, demonic. For where envy and self-seeking exist, confusion and every evil thing are there. But the wisdom that is from above is first pure, then peaceable, gentle, willing to yield, full of mercy and good fruits, without partiality and without hypocrisy. Now the fruit of righteousness is sown in peace by those who make peace. Where do wars and fights *come* from among you? Do they not come from your desires for pleasure that war in your members?

When our minds are set on the things of the world, on greed, on sexual immorality, the lusts of the flesh, what happens is our free will becomes attached to those things. Our will gets attached to those patterns of life. But when we don't conform to the world, and we conform instead to the Word of God, and are transformed by the renewing of our mind. It is our job to move our will into the will of God. We are no longer taking our path in life, we are taking the path of God's Word. We live in a way where His Word is a lamp unto our feet. We are no longer on the broad road which leads to destruction, which many find, but instead we are on the narrow road, which is short and straight, and few find it. That is what we do, we move our will out of the way and we find the narrow road which is the will of God.

Say this out loud,

God's will is His Word and His Word is His will.

You must understand that God's Word is His will. That is why it says in the gospels that Jesus was righteously indignant at the leper when the leper came and asked him, "If you're willing, you can make me well," and Jesus said, "I am willing. Be well." Jesus was the express image, the visible image of the invisible God. He rebuked Philip when he said to him in John 14:9,

Jesus saith unto him, Have I been so long time with you, and yet hast thou not known me, Philip? he that hath seen me hath seen the Father; and how sayest thou then, Show us the Father?

We study the life of Jesus and how Jesus walked out the will of God on the earth, and we know Jesus is the will of the Father. The Word is the will of the Father. So it is our job to transform our minds, with the renewing of our mind, to bring our will into alignment with God's will. We do this by not setting our minds on the things of the flesh but on the things of the Spirit. It is our job to set our minds on the things of the Spirit. Remember Deuteronomy 30:15 says,

See, I set before you today life and prosperity, death and destruction.

This scripture shows us that there are only two paths in life. There is a path that leads to blessing and eternal life, which is the way, the truth, and the life, in Jesus Christ, or there's a path of destruction: cursing, sin, eternal damnation, and death. It's up to us to renew our mind, to get our will into God's will. When you find God's will for your life, you stay in the confines of God's Word, you will only go up in life!

I asked an evangelist friend of mine, "What is the deepest, most powerful revelation you've ever received?" and he replied, "The most powerful revelation I've ever received was when I read Deuteronomy 28, and how it said that you will only go up and not down. You will always be the head and never the tail." He said, "When that revelation hit my spirit, and I knew that it was true, my life has only gone in an upward trajectory. Even when trials come, even when struggles arise, even when things show up in life, they flee just as fast as they show up! And as they flee, my life has gone in an upward trajectory ever since." Because he took his life and aligned his life with the will of God, he realized that he would always be the head and never the tail. And that's what I've experienced in my own life as well!

I want you to say this out loud and believe it,

I am responsible for my mind. I am responsible for my mind.

You've probably heard this before, but I want it to be real to you. You are responsible for your mind. Maybe you've never heard this before. They don't teach this in a lot of churches. A lot of churches will teach you that you are a product of your mind, that you can't control your mind. They'll put you on medications, they'll get you on antidepressants or anti-anxiety medication. They will get you on this pill, on that pill. They will get you on everything except for the Jesus Pill! They'll make you think that you are a slave to your mind, but that's not true! You possess your mind, your mind does not possess you.

I'm going to reiterate, you are a spirit, an eternal being. You possess a soul, which is your mind, your will and your emotions. And you live in a body. You possess your soul, your soul does not possess you. You are in charge, and responsible for your will. Your will is not responsible for you. You are responsible for your soul. When you take on responsibility for your mind, for your intelligence, for your wisdom, for your knowledge, for your free will and for your emotions, it eliminates your ability to be a victim in life. That is humbling for a lot of people, and especially people in my generation. You will see a lot of young people who don't want to take responsibility for their minds because it has become their identity. They've allowed depression, anxiety, and defeat. Victimization, and the attention it gets from people, leads them to make victimhood a part of their identity, instead of living a victorious life. They've chosen to live as a victim. But I want you to know right now, you do not have to live as a victim in this life! We haven't even gotten deep yet we've just covered basic topics, but you can live as the Bible says, as more than a conqueror through Christ, who gives you strength! You can live as a victorious servant of the living God.

Jesus said, in Matthew 11:28,

Come unto me, all *ye* that labour and are heavy laden, and I will give you rest. Take my yoke upon you, and learn of me; for I am meek and lowly in heart: and ye shall find rest unto your souls.

He said, "I'll give you rest for your soul, for your mind, for your will, for your emotions. I'll give you the Kingdom of God, the righteousness, peace and joy in the holy ghost, where you'll live as a victorious Christian all the days of your life!" All the days of your life, you do not have to live as a victim. As you are reading this right now I prophesy over your life,

From this day forward, you will not live another day as a victim. You will live every day as a conqueror in Jesus's name.

We are responsible for our mind. Practically speaking, what does that mean? There are five things you're responsible for. These five things I want you to get in your spirit. Number one, you are responsible for what gets in your mind. This means you are responsible for what you watch, and you're responsible for what you listen to. What you watch and what you listen to will eventually become your thoughts, so you are responsible for what gets in your mind.

Number two, you are responsible for how you think. Remember, your mind does not have control of you, you have control of your mind. That's why the bible says in 2 Corinthians chapter 10 that we pull down every imagination that attempts to exalt itself above Christ. When lies try to pop up, when evil thoughts show up in your life, we tear them down using the Word of God. We make them obedient to what God says about us.

Number three, you are responsible for what you feel. Because what you watch, what you listen to, turns into what you think, and what you think turns into how you feel, you are responsible for what you feel. Again, because you are responsible for what gets in your mind, you are responsible for what you think, and because what you think is responsible for how you feel, you are responsible for what you feel.

Number four, you are responsible for what you speak. That is why Jesus said in Matthew 12:38

For by your words you will be justified, and by your words you will be condemned.

And lastly, number five, you are responsible for what you do. When you understand that you are responsible for these five things, you will take authority over them, according to the blood of Jesus, and according to the Word. As you plead the blood and you speak the Word, you declare the Word, you become the Word. It will shine out from you, from glory to glory, with unveiled face. Just like Paul wrote, as God's Word gets inside of you, through what you listen to and read, and you meditate on it, the Word becomes what you think. And as it becomes what you think, it will be what comes out of your mouth. And as it comes out of your mouth, it will be what creates your path in line with the perfect will of God. It is what prophesies your destiny. It's what creates victory in your life.

This is why the bible says in 2 Corinthians 4:13,

It is written: "I believed; therefore I have spoken." Since we have that same spirit of faith, we also believe and therefore speak.

In order to align with God's will for your life, you must believe His Word. You must hear His Word, believe His Word and speak His Word. Then it transforms your mind from the inside out. We are responsible for our minds, we are responsible for aligning our life with the will of God.

I want to debunk a lie that a lot of Christians fall into. A lot of Christians think that they can't know God's will for their life, but that's not true at all! You're actually expected to know God's will for your life. Ephesians 1:8-9 says,

Which He made to abound toward us in all wisdom and prudence, having made known to us the mystery of His will, according to His good pleasure which He purposed Himself...

I want you to say this out loud,

God has made His will known to me.

God has revealed the mystery of His will, in His Word. There is an old saying, "The gospels, Matthew, Mark, Luke, and John, were written *for* the church, but the epistles were written *to* the Church." So the epistles are the revelation of who you are now, as a born-again believer in this life. When you read the epistles, including what Paul wrote, you receive revelation of your identity in Christ. You find out God's will because the mystery of His will is revealed to you. It says He has made known to you the mystery of His will. So when you understand that the mystery of His will is made known to you, you can then align your life with the will of God.

Jesus is God's Will

You must draw a line in the sand and make sure that nothing ever trumps God's Word in your life. If there is any area of your life that doesn't align with the Word, you must immediately align your life with God's Word, or else you will be out of the will of God. That is what it means to be transformed by the renewing of your mind; aligning your life with God's will. Your will must be to do the will of God. Remember Jesus said in John 14:15,

If you love Me, you will keep My commandments.

Another key to renewing your mind, is to understand that the greatest love that you can show Jesus is to keep His Word. And that has been the common theme all throughout eternity. God told Abraham, "Listen to my voice. Don't depart from my Word. Meditate on it day and night. Don't go to the right or to the left." He told the same thing to Moses, the same thing to Joshua, and King David, the same thing.

Even Jesus, when He was praying in the Garden of Gethsemane, the Bible says that He sweat blood because He knew what torment He was going to go through as He went to the cross. But even Jesus, in His final prayer, said "nevertheless, not my will, but your will be done." Making your life a living sacrifice for the Lord is laying down your will and making the eternal decision to always align with the will of God, out of love for Jesus. You decide to say every day, "I love you, and I keep your commandments."

God's will must become our will. We love the Lord and we keep His Word. We keep his commandments and as you get God's Word in you, it transforms you from the inside out. All of a sudden your mind is not set on the things of this earth, but instead is set on the things of heaven. As your mind is set on the things above and not beneath, you become heavenly minded, and you'll naturally be led by the

Spirit of God. The Bible said Romans 8:14,

For as many as are led by the Spirit of God, these are sons of God.

God's Spirit wrote God's Word according to 2 Timothy 3:16 which says,

All Scripture *is* given by inspiration of God, and *is* profitable for doctrine, for reproof, for correction, for instruction in righteousness,

If you don't know God's Word, which is His will, then you won't be able to be led by the Spirit. Jesus is the expressed will of God. I want you to say that out loud,

Jesus is the will of God.

This means you can study the ministry and life of Jesus, every word Jesus spoke, every action Jesus took, every place Jesus went, and see exactly what the Father would do if He was here in the earth today. In John 6:38 Jesus says,

if you've seen me you've seen the father.

Colossians 1:15 says,

He is the image of the invisible God, the firstborn over all creation.

The Bible says here that Jesus is the expressed image of God in the earth. So in order to know God's will for your life, you must know God's will in general first. What is God's will? The life of Jesus. The Bible says in Acts 10:38,

How God anointed Jesus of Nazareth with the Holy Spirit and with power, who went about doing good and healing all who were oppressed by the devil, for God was with Him.

Jesus healed everyone, all who were oppressed by the devil. This means if there is any oppression in your life, Jesus has already paid the price for it. You have the authority, by the blood of Jesus, to kick the devil out of your town. out of your life forever. You plead the blood of Jesus, submit to God, you resist the devil, and the Bible says he will flee from you.

You know that it is God's will to heal everybody. You know it is God's will for you to prosper. You know it is God's will for you to have an easy yoke and a light burden. You know it is God's will to give you rest. You know it is God's will to give you abundant life. You look at the words Jesus spoke and the actions that He took, because He is the expressed image of the invisible God. The Bible says in John 8:36,

Therefore if the Son makes you free, you shall be free indeed.

Your life should be free! If there is any bondage in your life, then that is not God's will for your life. God's will is for you to be totally free. 1 John 3:8 says,

He who sins is of the devil, for the devil has sinned from the beginning. For this purpose the Son of God was manifested, that He might destroy the works of the devil.

By studying the life of Jesus and His ministry in God's Word we can see clearly what is God's will. God's will for your life is exactly how Jesus walked on the earth. Galatians 5:1 says,

Stand fast therefore in the liberty by which Christ has made us free, and do not be entangled again with a yoke of bondage.

Christ has set you free, to anoint you with the Holy Ghost and with power, to go around doing good! Mark 16:17 says,

And these signs will follow those who believe: In My name they will cast out demons; they will speak with new tongues...

Because you are free in Christ you will move mountains with your faith. You will watch them be cast up and thrown into the sea. You will raise the dead. You will cleanse the leper. You will cast out devils everywhere you go. You are the light of the world. When you start getting the Word of God in you, it changes your will, your ability to choose, into the will of the Father. The day you died to sin and were born again, your will went out the window. Your life is now presented as a living sacrifice to the Lord. Galatians 2:20 says,

I have been crucified with Christ; it is no longer I who live, but Christ lives in me; and the *life* which I now live in the flesh I live by faith in the Son of God, who loved me and gave Himself for me.

A dead man has no will. Say this out loud,

It is not my will that goes forth, but the Father's will.

God's will for your life will always supersede your will for your life. Amen! I want you to say this out loud,

I will fulfill God's will for my life in Jesus mighty name! I will fulfill God's will for my life!

You are not going to be another Christian that runs around like a chicken with your head cut off, unsure of God's plan and will for your life. You are responsible for your mind and what gets in your mind. You are responsible for what you think. You are responsible for how you act. You are responsible for what you speak. It is time to put on big boy pants and big girl pants, and walk in the victory that Jesus paid for with His blood! To be more than a conqueror in this life. To let your faith fill you up, to move mountains and to go and live a victorious life by the blood of Jesus.

The Bible says in 1 John 4:17,

Love has been perfected among us in this: that we may have boldness in the day of judgment; because as He is, so are we in this world.

Hallelujah! Praise the Lord! You are responsible for your life. Nobody else. God's Word getting inside of you creates a light before your feet, a lamp to your path, and you'll have good success everywhere you go! Joshua 1:1 shows us what God says about plugging in with His Word and His will,

After the death of Moses the servant of the LORD, the LORD said to Joshua son of Nun, Moses' aide: "Moses my servant is dead. Now then, you and all these people, get ready to cross the Jordan River into the land I am about to give to them—to the Israelites. I will give you every place where you set your foot, as I promised Moses. Your territory will extend from the desert to Lebanon, and from the great river, the Euphrates—all the Hittite country—to the Mediterranean Sea in the west. No one will be able to stand against you all the days of your life. As I was with Moses, so I will be with you; I will never leave you nor forsake you. Be strong and courageous, because you will lead these people to inherit the land I swore to their ancestors to give them.

"Be strong and very courageous. Be careful to obey all the law my servant Moses gave you; do not turn from it to the right or to the left, that you may be successful wherever you go. Keep this Book of the Law always on your lips; meditate on it day and night, so that you may be careful to do everything written in it. Then you will be prosperous and successful. Have I not commanded you? Be strong and courageous. Do not be afraid; do not be discouraged, for the LORD your God will be with you wherever you go."

The Bible says that your path is your responsibility your, destiny is your responsibility. God has plans for you, He knew you before you were in your mother's womb. He kneaded you together, with plans to prosper you, and never to harm you. To give you a hope and to give you a future. But it is your responsibility to get God's Word inside of you, to get fiery preaching inside of you, to spend time with the Lord in fasting and prayer. Find out God's will for your life and conquer that will with everything inside of you, and then you'll have good success everywhere you go. God's given you everything that you'll ever need to grab a hold of His Word and to find out His will for your life and as you walk in it you will prosper in all that you do God is backing you

Aren't you thankful that we have the ability to choose? We have the ability to choose *this* day life, and blessing, hallelujah! We have this day to choose the blessing of the Lord, to walk according to His Word, to choose to obey His will for our Life and to shine brighter and brighter until the full peak of day. What a beautiful thing! Hallelujah! Praise the Lord!

Feel Like Walking Like Jesus

In Romans 12:2 Paul said,

And do not be conformed to this world, but be transformed by the renewing of your mind, that you may prove what *is* that good and acceptable and perfect will of God.

This means that when you see things going one way in the world, it is our job to actually go the entire opposite direction that everybody else in the world is going. But there's only one way to do that and you can't do it in your own strength. It has to be done by renewing your mind according to God's Word. You can harness your emotions and force them to align with God's Word. I want you to say this out loud,

I am in control of my emotions.

You can talk to just about any professor in psychology or any therapist, any scientist, or even to a lot of pastors today, who will tell you that you are not in control of your mind. But that is totally incorrect. You are 100% in control of your mind, and if your mind controls you, then that is wrong. You were never created to be controlled by your mind. God gave you your mind, He gave you your soul, your will and your emotions, for you to control. Your mind is a tool given to you by God to live and function on the earth as God functions. It's actually the vessel that God uses to work through you. That's why your mind must be renewed according to the Word of God.

You will talk to a lot of different therapists, phycologists, all these different people and they will tell you that you need to be on different medication. You need to be on this medication, that medication, go see Big Pharma, do your breathing ritual, go to your yoga class, do your stretching, do all of these worldly things in order to bring your mind in control. But the reality is you have the authority to put your mind under control. There is not one emotion that you will ever experience in life that you are not in control of. Your emotions are a byproduct of what is inside of you. Your emotions are the overflow of what is in your heart, what is in your mind and how you view yourself and your life. You are responsible for your emotions

When your mind starts acting up, when lies start coming your way, it is your job as a Christian, when you're born-again, a new creation, to bring your mind under control. And remember, you do it by the Word of God and through the power of God's Spirit.

Your soul is a culmination of your mind, your intelligence, your will, your ability, to choose, and your emotions. Once you realize God's intelligence is available to you, you will start to tap into the knowledge and wisdom that is in God's Word. Once you tap into that, you will realize that your ability to choose is under your control. You will choose, as God would have you to choose, His perfect will for your life. Once you've decided, "I want God's will for my life," now you are in a position where you can learn how to put your emotions in submission to your spirit. Put your emotions into submission to your spirit so everything flows in one order, going in one direction, for the advancement of the Kingdom of God.

First, we want to live a life at full capacity in God's knowledge, in God's wisdom. When you carry the knowledge and the wisdom of God then you will have the same results as those that have in the past.

For example, King Solomon carried the wisdom of God. Not only was He the wisest man to ever walk the earth, outside of Jesus of course, but he was the richest. Wisdom brings wealth. When you walk in the wisdom of God you will ultimately walk in the wealth that God has prepared for you ahead of time

Secondly, God will give you sufficient knowledge so that you don't perish in life. Hosea chapter 4:6 says,

My people are destroyed for lack of knowledge. Because you have rejected knowledge, I also will reject you from being priest for Me; Because you have forgotten the law of your God, I also will forget your children.

So when you don't lack in knowledge you won't perish. You will have a firm foundation. You will live successfully. You will go from glory to glory, victory to victory, strength to strength in your life. You'll actually be somebody that God uses to be a leader to lead His sheep. That is the result of God's intelligence in your life.

Now, renewing your mind according to God's will in your life, gives you freedom to choose and to walk this life as Jesus walked. Remember He said in John 14:15,

If you love Me, keep My commandments.

We show God our love to Him by keeping walking and obeying His Word. By loving God, and walking according to His Word, which is His will, we will then walk as Jesus walked in the earth. I don't know about you, but I want to walk as Jesus walk He said, "when I leave you will do these same works that I do, and even greater works than these." I want you to say this out loud,

I will do even greater works in Jesus' name!

When you commit in your mind to do the will of God, you will do the works of God. I don't want someone religious person getting their panties in a wad here. God will do the works *through* you. You will be the vessel that God uses to do His works in the earth.

Learning how to harness your emotions is crucial in renewing your mind to do the Will of God. This teaching will change your life forever! The number one way to control your emotions is to learn how to rejoice always, guarding your joy. Philippians chapter 4:4 says,

Rejoice in the lord always Again I say rejoice.

Rejoicing is actually the key to pushing out carnal emotions. I want you to say that out loud,

Rejoicing is the way I push out carnal emotions

This is why the Bible says in Isaiah 61:3,

To console those who mourn in Zion, To give them beauty for ashes, The oil of joy for mourning, The garment of praise for the spirit of heaviness; That they may be called trees of righteousness, The planting of the LORD, that He may be glorified."

When you put on the garment of rejoicing, the garment of praise, you force out carnal emotions like sadness, anxiety, and depression. That's why it says in Psalm 100:4,

Enter into His gates with thanksgiving, *And* into His courts with praise. Be thankful to Him, *and* bless His name.

When you are in a constant place of gratitude, thankfulness, and rejoicing, it pushes out carnality and heaviness in your life. If you keep reading, the Bible says in Philippians 4:4,

Rejoice in the Lord always. Again I will say, rejoice! Let your gentleness be known to all men. The Lord *is* at hand. Be anxious for nothing, but in everything by prayer and supplication, with thanksgiving, let your requests be made known to God; and the peace of God, which surpasses all understanding, will guard your hearts and minds through Christ Jesus.

Paul actually gives you a remedy or a prescription to always live in the peace of God that surpasses knowledge. The scripture says, "Don't be anxious about anything, but in everything by prayer and supplication with thanksgiving let your requests be made known to God." When anxiety tries to move into your life, stress tries to move into your life, the spirit of fear tries to move into your life, you say, "No!" You kick it out by first rejoicing, then by prayer and supplication, which is the act of standing in the gap, understanding that it's going to be done. God is bringing forth what you've already asked! Mark chapter 11:24 says,

Therefore I say to you, whatever things you ask when you pray, believe that you receive *them*, and you will have *them*.

When it seems like there's an impossible situation, rise up and rejoice. Rejoice that you are more than a conqueror! That every mountain moves as you pray, that as words come out of your mouth, they are a lamp to your feet, that God hears your prayers, that He is strong on your behalf. Start rejoicing and throwing up thanksgiving ahead of time, and you are guaranteed to have whatsoever you've asked for! He didn't say, "Ask for some things and I'll make sure to give them to you." He said, "*Whatever* you ask in my name, I will give them to you!" The literal translation of this scripture means, "If I don't have it already, I will make it for you." If He doesn't have it already, He will make it for you. If there is not already a way prepared for you, He will make a way for you. If the money is not already here, He will have it waiting for you there. He will make a way where there is no way. It is hard to be miserable while spending time worshiping at the throne in the presence of God.

Control your emotions and make them submit to the Spirit. Pray, walk in supplication, and give thanksgiving ahead of time by faith. When you do those things, it says the peace of God, which surpasses knowledge, will guard your heart. Rejoicing, giving praise, and praying and thanking God ahead of time that your answer is coming, guards your heart. It guards your mind. Rejoicing and praise, combined with prayer and thanksgiving, guards your heart and they guard your mind,.

Set Your Mind

Earlier in this book we discussed how important it is to understand that you are responsible for what gets into your mind. What you watch, what you listen to, ultimately determines what you think on, and what you think on ultimately determines how you feel, and how you feel ultimately determines what comes out of your mouth, and then what you do. To break it down, at the root, to catch it before anything evil ever even happens, you stay in a constant state of rejoicing and praising God for His works are good.

Further in Philippians 4, starting at verse 8 it says,

Finally, brethren, whatever things are true, whatever things are noble, whatever things are just, whatever things are pure, whatever things are lovely, whatever things are of good report, if there is any virtue and if there is anything praiseworthy – meditate on these things.

Say this out loud,

I am an optimist.

It is very easy to be somebody that always looks at the negative, to walk around like a negative Nancy. It is easy to be a negative Nancy. But it takes the spirit of faith to live a life of optimism. The world calls faith optimism, but the spirit of faith is not optimism. Faith is knowing, without a shadow of a doubt. Hebrews 11:1 says,

Now faith is the substance of things hoped for, the evidence of things not seen.

Faith is knowing the unknown, but you still know. You still know. Faith is always optimistic. Faith doesn't talk the same way that negative people talk. It doesn't look at circumstances the way that negative people look at circumstances. Faith sets its mind on whatever is true, whatever is honorable, just, pure, whatever is lovely, whatever is worthy of praise. That is what faith sets its mind on. Focus on the fact that you are going to heaven when you pass on from this life. It is hard to be miserable when you are too busy praising God. Thanking Him for already bringing you as far as you are now, and that you know that He is the same God that is in the Bible. He's a rewarder of those who seek him.

He will always make a way. If He is able to deliver the Israelites out of Egypt, He will deliver you out of wherever you are at. If He could split the Red Sea, put Noah on an ark, tear down a giant, drop the walls of Jericho, your minor problem is no issue for God. God could create the heavens and the earth in six short days Whatever is going on in your life, God needs six short seconds to flip it on its head for good. No matter where you are at, no matter what's going on. But you have to believe.

That is easy for me to sit here and to say to you, "Don't worry about it, you have nothing to worry about! You just pray, you supplicate, you rejoice, and God is coming through!" But it has to get inside of you, in your spirit. It has to be your heart posture. You have to know it in your knower. It has to be in you deep, in your innermost being. It has to be a part of you, so that no matter what, you can say, "If God be for me, who can be against me?" No matter what! *That* is the spirit of faith.

To guard your mind and to harness your emotions, you must think on these things. These things which are pure, which are lovely, which are true, which are honorable, whatever is commendable, and anything excellent or worthy of praise. Meditate on these things. Whatever you have learned and received and heard and seen in the Word, practice those things and the God of peace will be with you. We are responsible for what gets in our mind. We are responsible for what we think on. We are ultimately responsible for the result of our life.

People give too much credit to the devil for how their life turned out. The devil is not responsible for how your life turns out once you are born again. The Bible says that the devil is under your feet once you're a born-again Christian, and the power of God lives in you. Colossians 1:27 says,

To them God willed to make known what are the riches of the glory of this mystery among the Gentiles: which is Christ in you, the hope of glory.

The kingdom of God lives in you. You become fully responsible for the direction and destiny of your life, whether or not you fulfill God's will for your life. But I want to prophesy it over your life right now,

You are going to be somebody that fulfills God's will for your life. You are not going to miss it even a little bit. You are not going to go to the right, you're not going to go to the left. You are going to be so engulfed with God's Word and His presence, that you will live in the full, perfect will of God for you. You are going to go up, you are going to see victories, you are going to break the mold in your family. That generational curse, that addiction, that issue that's followed your family, sickness and disease, it won't touch you. It won't touch your kids. You are going to abide in the shadow of the almighty. Whatever you ask and believe you have received, you will receive it in Jesus's mighty name! You will fulfill the Word and will of God for your life.

2 Corinthians 10:3-4 says,

For though we walk in the flesh, we do not war according to the flesh. For the weapons of our warfare *are* not carnal but mighty in God for pulling down strongholds...

What are strongholds? Strongholds are in your mind. Strongholds are demonic oppression that hold your mind strongly. The most simple way to say it is, demonic influence has a strong hold on your mind, influencing the direction that your life is going, the way you believe, the way you think about yourself, the way you feel God. But you have been given weapons that aren't according to the flesh.

They are actually weapons to destroy and tear down those strongholds that have a strong hold on your mind. We destroy arguments and every lofty opinion raised against the knowledge of God. We take every thought captive to obedience to Jesus Christ.

To harness our emotions, we take every lie and every thought captive that goes against God's Word. Put them into alignment with God's Word. If a thought comes up that says you are too young, you are too old, you are too fat, you are too skinny, you are not anointed enough to do what it is God's called you to do, whatever it is, you bring it into alignment with God's Word. You say, "No. It doesn't matter what I look like, it doesn't matter where I've been, it matters where I'm going, and the Bible says that the same spirit that rose Jesus from the dead lives in me. That spirit is upon me, for He has anointed me to preach the gospel, to bring freedom to those that are oppressed, to bind up the brokenhearted."

Declare God's Word over your life. Speak it and get it into your ears. It builds your faith. It aligns your heart, your mind, your will, your emotions with what God's Word says and you will find your feet going where your words go. Your feet will always follow your eyes and your words. I want you to say this out loud,

My feet follow my eyes and my words.

Bishop David Oyedepo says, "If it's too big for your mouth, it's too big for your hand." If God's will for your life is too big for you to speak and declare, then it is too big for you to walk in. But if you are reading this right now, that is not the case for you. You know God's will for your life and it is not too big for your mouth, so you will speak it, you will declare it, and you will walk in it. Where your words go and where your eyes go, your feet will go. Everything that goes against the Word of God goes against the will of God.

Pay attention to any time you're feeling sorry for yourself. Brother Hagin used to say, "You know the devil's talking to you anytime you are feeling depressed, oppressed, anxious." Any time those thoughts come in, and you know that you're experiencing an emotion that you wouldn't experience in heaven, it's actually your job and responsibility to cast that ugly thing down to the pit of hell, and it

Never enters your life again. Praise the Lord! I'll give you one more example. Starting in James 1:2, the Bible says,

My brethren, count it all joy when you fall into various trials, knowing *this***, that the trying of your faith worketh patience. But let patience have** *its* **perfect work, that you may be perfect and complete, lacking nothing.**

In other words, rejoice when trials of different kinds come your way, because it actually creates the perseverance and the endurance of your genuine faith. Rejoice because you know you will be delivered. Rejoice when the storm comes your way because you know that you will cast it down. You will tell it to shut up, and be still. Rejoice when the mountain is in your way because it is an opportunity to use your faith to move it. Rejoice when there are enemies coming your way because you know they will scatter from you seven different ways! Rejoice when it seems like all hell is breaking loose because you know if God is for you, no one can be against you. You rejoice!

Align your emotions with the good report. I want you to say this out loud,

My emotions are aligned with the good report

In Numbers 13-14, it says that there were twelve spies sent out by Moses and Aaron, and amongst those twelve spies, were Caleb and Joshua. They went and scouted out the promised land, but in the promised land they saw that there were giants. There were Amalekites, there were Canaanites, there were all these wicked people, and they said, "We were as grasshoppers in their sight, the land is flowing with milk and honey, it's prosperous, it's everything God said it was, but they're so strong, there's no way we could take the land."

The Bible says that they spread this evil report of unbelief to the congregation of Israel. When you align your emotions with the good report, you'll never be deceived by the evil report of unbelief.

That is what optimism in the spirit of faith does. It keeps your mind constantly set on the good report, no matter what the circumstance. The Bible says that those families that believed the report of unbelief didn't get to enter into the promised land. Those who believed the evil report did not get to inherit the promised land. You set your mind on things above, not on things below.

Remember from before, the Bible says that the wisdom of mankind, human wisdom is sensual and demonic, and every wicked thing lives in that. So instead, we set our mind on things above. We know, no matter what, God will pull through. Just like Shadrach, Meshach and Abednego, the Hebrew children, who said, "We're not bowing down to you Nebuchadnezzar. We know for a fact our God can deliver us from your stupid fire. And even if he doesn't, who cares! We're going home to see Him. We'll go right to Abraham's bosom, we'll go get fat and sassy on the other side." That's how you have to look at life.

The Bible says in Proverbs 23:7,

As a man believes in his heart so is he

And because Caleb had a different spirit about him, the spirit of faith, he believed the good report, and he spoke it. Caleb said, "If God before us, we can surely overcome them! Let us go at once!" He believed God's report and he spoke it. That is the spirit of faith. Go to 3 John, verse 2, Paul said,

Beloved, I pray that you may prosper in all things and be in health, just as your soul prospers.

In other words, he prayed that our health would prosper even as our soul prospers. People get upset, "You preach that health and wealth gospel…" No, John did. He said in 3 John 1:3,

For I rejoiced greatly when brethren came and testified of the truth *that is* in you, just as you walk in the truth.

Paul said I want your health to prosper, *and* I want your soul to prosper, your mind your will and your emotions. I want every area of your mind to prosper. Your intelligence, your ability to choose your emotions. I want your mind to prosper in the Lord. That is why Paul told Timothy, "Don't be scared Timothy, God has not given us a spirit of fear, nor of timidity, anxiety, depression, heaviness, but He's given us a spirit of power and of love and a sound mind." That is what it looks like for your soul to prosper.

Wherever you are at right now, I want you to lift both hands up toward heaven and close your eyes, and I will pray for you.

Father in Jesus's mighty name, I command the mind of this person reading this book to prosper, every stronghold that's held them back, every heaviness, every anxiety, every depression, every wicked spirit from the pit of hell that's put a stronghold on their mind, I break it off now in Jesus's mighty name. Their mind is free. They will walk in power, love and the soundness of mind, and their soul will prosper all the days of their life in Jesus's mighty name.

God's Word will renew your mind to walk in His knowledge, in His wisdom, in His ability to choose what's right all the time, the blessing of God. You are in control of your mind and you are in control of your life. God's Word and God's anointing will make sure that your path is always straight and narrow, and it never gets crooked. The path will never get funny and it won't be the broad path that leads to destruction. Your life will go up and up, glory to glory, it will shine brighter and brighter to the very noon day, the peak of the day, in Jesus's mighty name! Hallelujah!

Partner With Us

If you have a desire to see the gospel get out and to see hungry kids fed, this is how you can partner with our ministry! Last year we reached 200 million people through social media and in-person evangelism, and this year we are believing God that we will reach even more people! I felt on my heart to feed a thousand kids this past Christmas, so we've joined with an organization called Feed The Hungry, who we partner with every month. Normally we feed 25 kids every day, and we are so excited to continue increasing our impact feeding the hungry!

I have a burden in my heart for Generation Z, to see Generation Z flipped upside down by the power of God! That they would be born again, renewed in their minds, and empowered to be mighty evangelists in the earth. When it seems like all hope is lost for Generation Z, I have a heart to watch God empower them to be the most radically passionate, on fire Christians, that this world has ever seen. So if you have a heart to see hungry kids get fed and you have a heart to see this ministry expand and keep reaching young people, this is how you can help out financially! Through Venmo, through Cash App, through Paypal, or on our website, revivalway.com and click partner financially today.

Venmo: @revivalway
Cash App: $revivalway
Paypal: @revivalway

I want to share this with you, because it's always good when you are giving faith to hang on to the promises of God. A couple of months ago I felt the Lord tell me to send $1,000 to a minister, and that it would create the next level in my financial progression as a ministry.

So I took $1,000 and I sent it to a minister. That was the most I'd ever given at one time before. It was personal too. So I took that thousand dollars and I sowed it into this pastor and ever since I sowed that seed I have watched this ministry explode financially. The Lord has blessed us tremendously! We've had a ton of monthly partners come and join the vision to see Generation Z shaken by the power of God, to see hungry kids fed. The Bible says in Galatians 6:7,

Do not be deceived, God is not mocked; for whatever a man sows, that he will also reap.

Whatever a man sows he also reaps. Because I sowed into another man's ministry, God in turn put it on people's hearts to sow into my ministry. And after giving that seed, I would say probably $10-15,000 have come in. Almost immediately, within just weeks, it started to flood into the ministry. And it's still coming in!

The Bible says I can expect an hundred-fold return. So $100,000 is making its way toward me. Put a demand on the promises of God! In 2 Corinthian 9:6 promises this return. Whoever gives a little bit, or only a small proportion of what you have, whoever sows sparingly or is stingy, will also reap sparingly. If you don't feel it leave your hand as you sow, you won't feel it come back as the harvest. But it says whoever gives bountifully, will also reap bountifully.

When you give to the advancement of the Kingdom of God, the point is to give with your heart attached to it. Jesus said where a man's money is, that is where his heart is also. God will test your heart with your money. Billy Graham used to say, "Give me five minutes with a man's checkbook, and I'll show you where his heart is." I love that quote! It says each one must give as they decide in their own heart. You have to decide how much you want to give, not reluctantly or under compulsion, because God loves a cheerful giver. The Bible says you don't give under compulsion or pressure. You don't give because I am here saying so, you have to give to the advancement of the Kingdom of God. Give joyfully!

Say this,

Lord, I'm so honored and privileged that I can financially bless this ministry and give to the advancement of your Kingdom.

God loves that! It's a sweet fragrance to the Lord. The Bible says in 2 Corinthians 9:8,

And God *is* able to make all grace abound toward you, that you, always having all sufficiency in all *things*, may have an abundance for every good work.

The Bible says He has distributed freely, He has given to the poor, His righteousness endures forever. He who supplies seed to the sower and bread for food will supply and multiply your seed for sowing and increase the harvest of your righteousness. So when you give and you're happy about it, to advance the Kingdom of God, God sees that and He takes notice of it. When He takes notice of it He advances your life. He puts special grace on you, He gives you special sufficiency, He pours out his power on you to advance what God's doing in your own life.

Think about Solomon. Everybody else was required to bring seven bulls and Solomon brought one thousand! Talk about an offering! What happened next? God revealed Himself to him and He said, "ask me anything." That's how much an offering moves the heart of God. He said, "You ask me anything and I'll do it for you Solomon." And he said, "I need wisdom to lead your people." God replied, "Not only will I give you wisdom, but I'm going to make you rich!" Solomon was already very rich, David was very rich, and Solomon was David's son. So Solomon was already very rich. But God said, "I will make you rich" and he made him the richest person on the planet ever in history by far. If you have a heart to advance the Kingdom and to see hungry kids fed and you want to give, right now is your time.

Let me bless you.

Father, in Jesus's mighty name, I thank you for the ability to be able to sow your Word, to preach your Word, and to impart wisdom and knowledge to these people. That they might be transformed by the renewing of their mind. Starting today, let the rest of their life never be the same. Their life will be built on the firm foundation which is your Word and they will see prosperity and success follow them all the days of their life, in Jesus's mighty name, amen.

Made in the USA
Coppell, TX
07 April 2022

76193384R00036